Blues at the End of the World

Blues at the End of the World

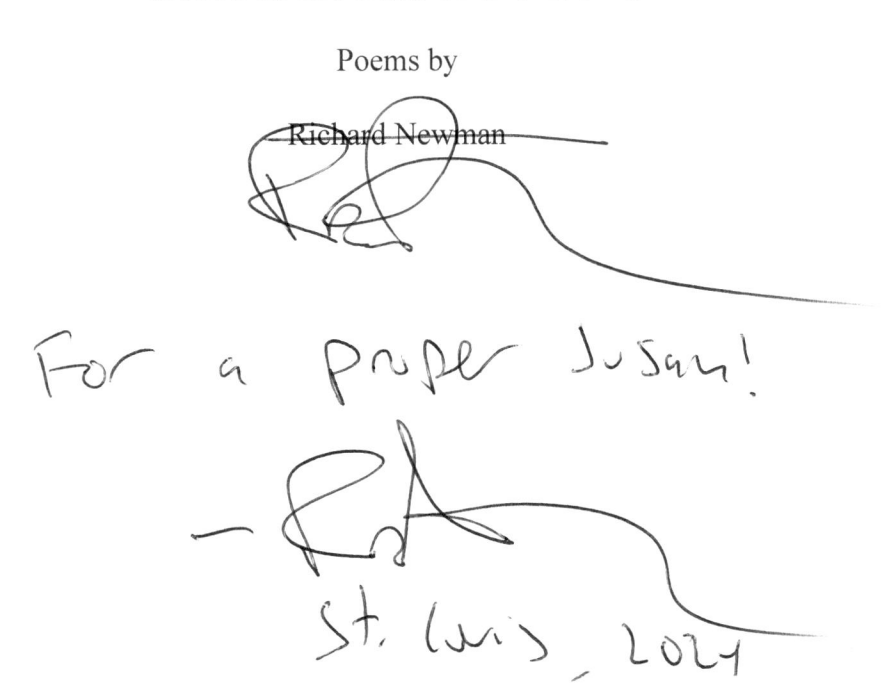

Poems by

Richard Newman

For a proper Susan!

— R

St. Louis, 2024

© 2024 Richard Newman. All rights reserved.
This material may not be reproduced in any form, published,
reprinted, recorded, performed, broadcast,
rewritten, or redistributed without
the explicit permission of Richard Newman.
All such actions are strictly prohibited by law.

Cover design by Shay Culligan
Cover image by Clare Rowntree
Author photo by Sayaka Goto

ISBN: 978-1-63980-508-2

Kelsay Books
502 South 1040 East, A-119
American Fork, Utah 84003
Kelsaybooks.com

for Sayaka and Genji

Acknowledgments

I am grateful to the editors of the following journals and anthologies where many of these poems originally appeared, sometimes in earlier versions with different titles.

American Journal of Poetry: "Bikini Nights, Independence Day," "Ode to Bui Vien, Saigon," "Ode to the Southeast Asian Bum Gun," "Responsory: Libera Me," "Vietnam Round"
The Book of Donuts (Terrapin Books, 2017): "Donut Tree"
Book of Matches: "Grave Scything in Takachiho," "Ode to the Chom Chom"
Bottle Rockets: "Tanka upon Getting Married"
Boulevard: "The Os after the Silence," "Plane Full of Soldiers," "Sleeping Sea"
Chestnut Review: "Last Weeks in Kamino, Japan"
Crab Orchard Review: "Donut Tree"
The Ekphrastic Review: "Passing through the Gates at Fushimi Inari Shrine"
Ghost City Review: "How to Take an Afternoon Nap in Southeast Asia"
Good River Review: "Petite chanson d'exile" (as part of "Trois chansons")
Haikuniverse: "Just Outside Saigon"
I-70 Review: "At a Homestay Near Tri Anh Lake, I Listen to the World Breathe," "Before Leaving Vietnam," "Bloat," "God of Majuro," "Hammock Song," "Home Islands," "Love Note," "No One on the Island Ever Complains about the Rain," "On a Road in Vietnam," "Smiling and Waving on Lunar New Year in Quỳnh Lưu, Vietnam"
Innisfree: "Beachcombers," "Grave Scything in Takachiho," "Milk"
Literary Matters: "Your Mother Still Sleeping, I Hold You Up to the Dawn"

New Madrid Review: "Please Describe Your Stay on the Island Property"
New Poetry from the Midwest 2017 (New American Press, 2017): "The Os after the Silence"
Noon: Journal of the Short Poem: "Ephemeral Tanka" (as "Majuro Tanka"), "Tanka a Month before Leaving Majuro"
Poetry East: "Hanoi Tour Guide Song"
Ribbons: Tanka Society of America Journal: "Birthday Tanka"
Tar River Poetry: "Dauber"
Trove: "Island Love Poem," "New City, Vietnam"
Valparaiso Poetry Review: "The Godless Month"
Verse Daily: "Plane Full of Soldiers"

Thanks to all the friends and family who have helped with this book, either from suggestions or support: Ned Balbo, Scott Berman, Steve Berti, Karen Brock, Sara Burge, Richard Cecil, Houda El Filali, Derek Elliot, Katja Zvan Elliot, Matthew Geers, Ginger, Juliana Grey, John Helden, Kelly Tarla Lorennij, Travis Mossotti, Jenny Mueller, Kerry and Ricki Newman, Erin Quick, Stefene Russell, Chris Roper, Steven D. Schroeder, Chris Taylor, Catherine Tufariello, Maryfrances Wagner, David Wilbanks, and Arian Wildschut. Most special love and appreciation for Sayaka Goto, Shanie Latham, Natalie Summers Newman, and Genji Goto Newman.

Contents

Paradise Blues

Sleeping Sea	15
No One on the Island Ever Complains about the Rain	17
Home Islands	19
Ephemeral Tanka	21
Donut Tree	22
Island Love Poem	24
Please Describe Your Stay on the Island Property	25
Birthday Tanka	27
Bikini Nights, Independence Day	28
God of Majuro	29
Tanka a Month before Leaving Majuro	31
Bloat	32
An Island Elegy	33
Tanka upon Leaving Majuro	35

Samurai Blue

Plane Full of Soldiers	39
Love Note	40
Passing through the Gates at Fushimi Inari Shrine	41
Grave Scything in Takachiho	42
The Os after the Silence	44
Abandoned Shinto Shrine in Kamino	45
The Best Unagi in Takachiho	46
Chicken Sashimi	47
Responsory: Libera Me	48
The Godless Month	49
Tanka upon Getting Married	50
Small Mirror on the Kitchen Table	51
Last Weeks in Kamino, Japan	52

Land of the Blue Dragon

Hammock Song	57
Hanoi Tour Guide Song	59
Ode to the Southeast Asian Bum Gun	60
How to Take an Afternoon Nap in Southeast Asia	61
At a Homestay Near Tri An Lake, I Listen to the World Breathe	63
On a Road in Vietnam	64
Ode to Bui Vien, Saigon	65
New City, Vietnam	67
Tanka Blessing for Our Baby, Not Yet Born	69
Ode to the Chom Chom	70
Milk	71
Petite chanson d'exile	73
Vietnam Round	74
Dauber	75
Smiling and Waving on Lunar New Year in Quỳnh Lưu, Vietnam	76
Before Leaving Vietnam	78
Your Mother Still Sleeping, I Hold You Up to the Dawn	79
Beachcombers	80

Magna Est Veritas

Here in this little Bay,
Full of tumultuous life and great repose,
Where, twice a day,
The purposeless, glad ocean comes and goes,
Under high cliffs, and far from the huge town,
I sit me down.
For want of me the world's course will not fail:
When all its work is done, the lie shall rot;
The truth is great, and shall prevail,
When none cares whether it prevail or not.

—Coventry Patmore

On a branch
floating downriver
a cricket, singing.

—Issa (translated by Jane Hirshfield)

Paradise Blues

*I must be crazy
not to have gone crazy here
in this crazy place.*

Sleeping Sea

Each new day hatches from a rooster's throat.
Halfway through its life,
it snoozes in the sand with dogs.

Beyond my hammock, the sea
sleeps, too, this afternoon, tucked in
between beaches at low tide.

The sea dreams of new canyons and continents,
the creatures that crawled from its reaches
a million years ago and sometimes return.

The sea dreams that shadows of ghost ships
caress its dusty floors.

When we dream of a calm sea it means
serenity and melancholia.

When the sea dreams calmly of us,
we can expect storms, king tides, tsunamis.

The sea dreams of the moon and us
bounding on the moon. The sea dreams
of the creatures it spawned launching out
to other worlds covered with other seas,
and those seas in turn dreaming of it.

In its sleep, the sea chews sunken ships,
refrigerators, car batteries.

The sea is sick but sleeping peacefully
this afternoon. It swells in its sleep
and licks salt onto the shore.

The sea slaps itself awake
with larger and larger waves
as the sun dribbles color on its waters.

Each day dies in the throats of dogs
barking and chewing it to pieces.

No One on the Island Ever Complains about the Rain

Like most people and animals, each rainstorm
has a soul, which it keeps in a furry pocket.

Some rains have short lives, small islands
of rain floating in sunny days.
Their long windblown hairs
shimmy in the sun a few moments
then steam to the heavens.

Other storms sulk in, sluggish and slow,
suck all the color from the world
but gray. A dog's bark
scratches through their drizzle
unable to strike any heat.

Some die before crossing the island.
Some ride the western winds,
taking with them smoke from fires
and Sunday plans.

When storms pass, they leave
tatters of their souls as dirty puddles.

Some rainstorms mist invisible
except for a few grape-sized drops
ripening from the porch roof.

One sunny day, a rain cloud followed
a friend all over the island, east
to west, ocean side to lagoon side.
No one who lived through an island drought
would call this personal storm anything
but lucky.

This morning, before the day rumbled in
on the first taxis and container trucks,
a storm had ghosted onto the island.
Hundreds of tiny hands tried to slip
though my windows, under the front door.
Shudders of rain curtained my porch.
The storm hadn't quite washed
the last scraps of sleep from my head,
but I was awake enough to know
that the storm had followed me
all the way from Missouri.

I longed for my soul to be part of something
larger. I wanted my soul to merge
with the storm's in the rattle on my tin roof.

I dozed. I indulged in that storm,
embraced its luck, looked forward
to its return. Before I'd stretched
out of bed to brew my tea, the storm
had ghosted out as quickly as it came,
quiet as the day had drifted in
on a frigatebird's wing, leaving the world
cold and damp and almost new.

Home Islands

From our outrigger, a boy points
to blue nothing on the horizon—Arno,
his home island, though he has never
sunk feet into the powder-milk sands
where his ancestors lie buried
and where he too will lie buried.

Some Marshallese will never reach
their home islands because of Castle Bravo,
Castle Romeo, king tides, or sea-level rise.

Many of us spend our whole lives
losing and finding them.
I lost mine a decade ago.
I'd suspected it was sinking.

Roughly the same cells in roughly
the same order rose to form
roughly the same self each morning,
a self drifting in uncharted doldrums.

During meetings or family reunions
with my now ex-in-laws, I often
retreated to a private island named
My God You People
Have No Inner Lives—
a place I was not proud
to inhabit for long.

Curious and without hope, I left
St. Louis after thirty years for this strand
of reef and sand in the Pacific.
I don't expect my home island
will suddenly bob to the surface.

We skim across the lagoon,
its infinite shades of blue harmonizing,
blues with no names, blurring
into sky, as if these blues are rising
to take back this borrowed atoll,
which of course they are.

Ephemeral Tanka

Here on the island,
time is faster, more cruel.
Ceilings rot. Knives rust.
My belt hangs green, sheathed with mold.
Sure, I'm next. Then this tanka.

Donut Tree

At most a ukulele, a basketball,
maybe a flip-flop above the rising tide,
we queue on sand this morning at Donut Tree
for coffee, vodka, SPAM sushi, and yes,
donuts, while poverty sprawls on either side
like a sleeping dog,

and when not sleeping, the mongrels of Majuro
would rather chase a running pair of knees
than gnaw old bones. Consumed by hunger, madness,
and mange, they've grown too many, and no one on
this island hasn't been attacked, most bitten,
as was my sweet mutt Ginger, so any dog
without a collar will be rounded up,
throats slit like pigs, feeding the Majuro
police force and their families for weeks.

Ginger and I walked down to City Hall,
a mostly open-air building, to buy
a five-buck tag that fastens to her collar.
The clerk behind the counter couldn't change
a $20. "Can you come back tomorrow?" she asked.
"Will you have change tomorrow?" I asked. She laughed.
At least I now had time for Donut Tree
before our weekly college lit mag meeting,
and our attendance would be doubled since
students magically know when I have donuts.

In any other place, these donuts—hard,
unglazed, unsprinkled in brown paper bags
Rorschached with grease stains—might be tossed for rats,
but here on Majuro, they take the shape
of our atoll, where the hole is our lagoon,

the glorious blue center of this life,
and everything around it is moist bonus,
and if I take two bags to Liberal Arts,
they will be gone in minutes, and Jae, our small
Korean Marxist geographer, will eat
a whole bag on his own, and now, my turn
in line, I know, not seeing any bags
but only smelling thick, delicious air
of deep-fat sugar-dough, that they've sold out,
again, the last bag left
the counter hours ago, and this has happened
four of the last five times I've visited
the Donut Tree, and I am once again
left with the hole, the fragrant nothingness
implying donut, and this is why these donuts
are so delicious—because they're sweet and rare,
because the Donut Tree's a lottery
we only savor if we're lucky, because
sometimes in this sad but carefree place,
only emptiness feeds our emptiness.
Crossing the coral rubble ocean side,
we stand on crumbling graves emptied by waves
and squint into the wind, the blurred horizon,
a ukulele above the rising tide.

Island Love Poem

Here love erupts from a blue void,
resolved to form its own island.

Locals sing of island love, words and harmonies
dying in the winds, which makes them laugh.

Love on a tropical island takes root
in a day and thrives like madness.
It can wither in a week.

Island love shifts slow as a sandy beach
because here there is no time.

When love wounds us, the saltwater cleanses,
and tides offer up new love.

There is only one love for each person on an island,
and those who find it are lucky.

Love can drift for thousands of miles,
take root and grow in coral rubble.

Some days, island love needs to rest in the shade and do nothing.

Island love is nocturnal. It steps out boldly
when hens stop clucking and roosters stop crowing.

On an island everyone knows who you will love before you do.
And they know who you should never love.

Please Describe Your Stay on the Island Property

We thought we had the island to ourselves.
The second story of the old house

reverberated like a log drum. Ear
to floorboards, I lay awake

listening to rain tumble on the tin roof
like rapids, like an amplified bloodstream.

The claws of a thousand hermit crabs
clicked delicately on the floors and walls.

Somewhere in the rafters a rat clicked too.
Sayaka tiptoed across the floor

and the whole house shuddered.
Neither of us could find a scrap of sleep

in the breeze, though we came here
to escape the tides of Majuro.

I heard every heartbeat in the house, throbbing, throbbing,
as the wind and rain whisked across the lagoon.

I heard the heartbeats of children
who ran through this house a generation ago.

A gust of wind made the whole house swing,
a spiderweb flutter in the eaves.

Sayaka's breathing next to me was like
a sack of sighs. Maybe they were my sighs.

Again and again, waves hurled themselves
against the beach, making the whole reef thrum.

The entire atoll hummed in an empty key.
Sleep lay further away than the nearest continent.

I was tired. Love was tired. Night was wide awake,
sucking the salty sea from the island's breast.

Birthday Tanka

Old poetry book for kindling,
the campfire approves.
52 loops round the sun—
we plot our next chapter.
Me: new tea in an old cup.

Bikini Nights, Independence Day

67 atom bombs blew us off our islands. Tonight across the Pacific, Americans celebrate their independence, bombs bursting in air. "A soldier told us our lives were smaller than a fingernail. They used us as human guinea pigs," said John Anjain, Rongelap magistrate. "There are only 90,000 people out there, who gives a damn," said Henry Kissinger. Godzilla hatched from Castle Bravo's 15 megatons, 1,000 times greater than Hiroshima and Nagasaki. In 1968 the US told us Bikini was safe, but the coconut crabs and breadfruit were radioactive, so we gave birth to jellyfish. Our children died of cancer. "With proper tactics, nuclear war need not be as destructive as it appears," said Henry Kissinger. On the home island we've never seen except in documentaries, a radioactive crab eats a radioactive coconut and hides itself in radioactive sand. Most of us don't remember how to fish or catch crabs. We live on canned mackerel and SPAM. The US has paid $125 million in reparations, $75 million over the last 15 years. Unemployment on Majuro is 40%. Worldwide, Godzilla has grossed $993,660,532 in movies alone.

Fingernail of moon
still glows orange in the night sky
from Castle Bravo.

God of Majuro

*For since the creation of the world, His invisible attributes,
His eternal power and divine nature, have been clearly seen,
being understood through what is made . . .*
                                       —Romans 1:20

A few parishioners slump
on plastic chairs beneath an awning.
A squat man in huge glasses gurgles
into a microphone that God is invisible,
He is all around us, and we should fear Him
and thank Him, repent and be free of sin.
With a broken umbrella, I am trying
to fight other dogs off from Ginger
when, from my back pocket, Siri repeats
"free of sin" and asks, "What can I help you with?
Go ahead, I'm listening."

Perhaps the gurgling man is right
and God is everywhere, even
against my left cheek, and as I walk home
with Ginger tugging toward the dogs behind us,
I consider that God could be the pull
of the leash and the push of coming rain,
and if God is the pulse
that bursts through in flower,
then God is the blooming of tumors
in my friend's intestines. And if God
is the sunlight that nuzzles a child's face,
then God is the shadow winging across
a young mind contemplating suicide.

We make it home before the rain,
which whistles round the house and streams
like a beaded curtain from our tin roof.

Our beach has flooded. Sayaka and I
sip tea and read in silence, waves
swirling below our bungalow. We float
on a world of our own creation.

Tanka a Month before Leaving Majuro

Our days here dwindling,
we speed into the lagoon.
Our boat's shadow skims
the sea floor with eagle rays.
So have I moved through these days.

Bloat

Death sunned itself on the empty beach.

I'd thought it was a pig,
but it was an island dog
grinning in the sand at low tide,
skin so stretched with bloat
its fur looked sparse.

It wore a funeral shawl of flies.
The waves had caressed it all night long
before retiring back to the lagoon.

From my hammock, I watched the tide
approach again, teasing it, wanting it back.

At first I thought *I know that bloat,*
for I too have lain swollen with bitterness,
stubborn in the sand.

I was foolish. When high tide reclaimed
its love, I saw the dead dog laughing
in the surf, bloated with sunshine.
It broke free from the shore
and bobbed westward in the blue waves.
Untethered from everything,
it fed itself to colonies of crabs
and wide-eyed fish along the way.
Not even an aircraft carrier
could slow its journey now.

An Island Elegy

Andy the dog is dead.

Alas. Alack. A parasite full of fleas.

Surely the stupidest creature I've ever seen,
he often got his white-and-black flanks stuck
in our porch slats rather than go down three steps.

He smelled like dead rat, as did our porch where he slept.

Originally named Tala, Marshallese for dollar,
he wasn't worth a salt-greened nickel,
and he looked more like an Andy
but answered to neither.

And yet he answered to everything.
Never was a creature more eager to be owned.

He tried to follow us into taxis.
He followed us on walks, picking fights with other dogs,
then *yipe-yipe-yip*ing back to us to hide between our legs.

For a no-brain, he was brilliant.
We could walk out of a store miles away
or step out of a cab, and he'd be there waiting for us,
dripping smiles, wagging
his stupid corkscrew tail like a pig's,

sweet nuisance.

I've seen kids from the compound sugar-call him—
ever hopeful, he'd come to receive a kick or slap,
over and over.

Our dog Ginger avoided him.
Manju, the alpha dog,
chased him away every night.
I'm told someone from Flametree,
the bar down the street,
threw rocks at him
and chased him into the lagoon.
He was floating there next morning.

Often on moonless nights, someone's wailing wakes me.
The crescent of beach behind our bungalow attracts
grieving souls who call out to the sea in the dark.
I've never seen them, but often their keening
lasts hours, and I know they mourn
lost children or lovers as the ocean
laps up their grief, their tears,
wave upon wave,
salt to salt.

Not even his fleas will mourn him.
He died frightened and alone.

We knew he wouldn't last long in this world,
that he was too stupid, needy, annoying.
We knew each time we could no longer stand his smell
and chased him off the porch
that we'd feel guilty to find him dead,
when he would no more
cause a ruckus at dinner
and end up floating in the lagoon
without so much as a ripple,
wanted by nothing but the tide.

Tanka upon Leaving Majuro

I tossed my last key,
free to enter anywhere—
no house, car, office.
Home is where loved ones lie dead.
Home is the world before us.

Samurai Blue

*Abandoned shrines dot
the countryside. Wasp eggs stir
in silence: new gods.*

Plane Full of Soldiers

5:50 am, a week before Christmas.

Twice now the flight attendant has bid them sing
"The Army Goes Rolling Along,"
and so they do, standing at attention,
sounding less like a march than off-key dirge,
both times the back half of the plane
breathing their last notes before the front half.

We unenlisted applaud their service.

They wear fatigues, combat boots.
They are children, blooming with bravado and acne.
One soldier calls her father on her iPhone,
nervous since she's never flown before.
Others play handheld video games.

Finally, our turn for takeoff.

How many of us will be dead by return trip,
our seats filled by the living?
These kids soon shipped out to the Middle East
run far worse odds than the old couple next to me,
not talking but holding hands, gazing
out the window in silence.

As we ascend and dawn gathers more day,
blue builds upon blue—cascades of blue,
runway lights at dawn blue, smurf
and crystal blue, the blue of eighth-grade eye shadow,
positive home pregnancy test blue, prewashed
blue, ice cube in gin and tonic blue, back burner
at midnight blue, corpse in the morgue blue,
the richest blues of our protected skies.

Love Note

At one point, and I don't remember when—
for love, like spring, stirs over many nights—
I handed you my heart. It wasn't soft
and squishy but flat and dry. And not long after
you spent whole nights carefully folding it,
caressing creases with your fingertips,
until it formed a great blue heron and flapped
about the room, bumping walls and lampshades.
We slept beneath it, hand in hand till dawn.
Your warm touch shaped a mushroom rising through
the loam, a white tiger bounding over
a chain of silver cranes around our bed.
I'm not so crafty with my hands. For you
I made a rectangle, smudged with shiny words.
And then our hearts unfolded and lay still,
misplaced and shuffled into other papers.
Tonight another's heart beats in my bed,
and through the open window I watch my heart,
a brittle moth brushing against the moon.

Passing through the Gates at Fushimi Inari Shrine

after Sylvia Plath's "Crossing the Water"

Vermillion gates, vermillion sunset, two lovers in vermillion
    sneakers.
Do these same vermillion gates keep reshuffling up ahead of us?
Each gate opens to a million other gates, a million other worlds.

The sun sets over the mountain, its shadow stretching into night.
Shadows clutch at us to linger by their ancient shrines,
whose rough-hewn stones tremble with silence and neglect.

Even the dead have left these cities of the dead.
Alone, we keep climbing through more vermillion gates.
Fox gods grin at our naïveté: *foolish lovers!*

Toward the top, a gray lake found the mountain's only flatness.
How many lanes of the dead lead us to forgetfulness?
Our shoes break the spell of the forgotten dead.

Grave Scything in Takachiho

Obon: the week for cleaning family graves,
when ancestors revisit household shrines
and try to stir up guilt. Armed with small scythes,
the three of us ascend the mountain path
to graves that haven't been tended in years.
I wonder what the ancestors would make
of me, a twice-divorced American—
depends how hard I work. We scythe in silence
while micro-showers range, leveling grass
and weeds of Sayaka's father's family.
Her father has no grave. He wasn't liked.
A few charred bone fragments rest in a vase
now lost to years of clutter, maybe tossed.
The day after he died, Sayaka heard
her mother, Omma, sing for the first time
in decades, like she sings to herself now,
her voice soft and delicate as ash.

Our sickles whisper to the dead, my mind
adrift. Last week, after an hour on Skype,
the interviewer ended with "good luck."
I knew I didn't get the job—good luck
being a cordial notch above "fuck you."
When my mom emailed after I'd left the States,
"I hope you find what you're looking for. Good luck,"
I knew what it meant—the last I'd hear from her.
I pull and cut above these dead who aren't
my blood, who lived when we were enemies,
thousands of miles from where my own blood dwindles,
dies in the unforgiving sandy flats
of Southern Illinois. What does blood
mean anyway but food for mosquitoes,
a few dead ones stuck to our sweaty necks.

A toad escapes my blade. We re-pile stones
that toppled from the rains and shifting earth.
Omma stands. Her whispered song trails off.
At last our work is finished here. We swig
cool barley tea, bow to the ancestors:
"We did the best we could," we say. "Good luck!"

The Os after the Silence

"The rest is silence. O, o, o, o. [*Dies*]"
—*Hamlet,* Act V, Scene ii, variant from first folio

I've pried from our garden an O-shaped bone,
three fingers long and wide,
worm-licked and white as moon.
Picked up—the loam that held it crumbles away.
Put to my eye—I view the world through death.

Overheard one morning, a friend moaned
from the downstairs couch, her sorrow
stifled with cushions as she sobbed herself
awake—or back to sleep—dampening
my fake velvet with dozens of little Os.

The morning after a crash, we neighbor kids
snared a tire from ditchweeds and bloodied gems
of glass and dribbled it down the road, great thwacks
against the asphalt, a bouncing, rolling O
with nowhere to go but over hills of soy.

Chorus heaps on chorus, and after the last
chord cuts off the cascade, a young woman's
voice warbles out, frail O hoping to join
once more the refrain, the bobbing sea of song,
but no—her lips an O of pleasure and then,

at finding herself alone, no longer lost
in music but found by us, *oh no* of shame,
dark O covered by a hand but echoing
in our minds' ears longer than any song,
longer than laughter, her O for more, her O
to merge, her O to be lost on waves of O.

Abandoned Shinto Shrine in Kamino

Abandoned *jinja*—
the sign says the god has gone
to another shrine.
I play guitar on the steps.
Insects shriek. The river laughs.

The Best Unagi in Takachiho

We sit on the dais, legs
tucked under low tables,
the only customers
all week. Outside, the streets
and sidewalks are clean. No trash,
no children, permanently
closed storefronts. Inside,
the old woman busies
herself straightening placemats,
arranging menus, wiping
tables no one has used
though this is the heart of town.
Her husband stands at the grill,
the long cigarette ash
sticking from his mouth
like a spectral finger pointing
from the grave, suspended
precariously over the best
unagi in Takachiho.

Chicken Sashimi

My new wife's mother had arranged the table:
        chicken sashimi,
a staple here. Sure, braised outside, but raw
inside, enough to make my stomach sicken.
The Kyushu summers are incubator-hot,
        the kitchens steamy,
and though they said that poultry here is not
        like US chicken
but clean, I didn't think that I'd be able
to slide it in my mouth, let alone chew.

        Of course I thought
about the guy at St. Louis Mardi Gras,
wearing just tighty-whities tie-dyed blue.
        He placed his order,
slurring, smirking: one raw chicken filet,
chewing it down on his way out the shop.
        The butcher pleaded,
"You don't want to do that, honey! Stop!"
        but he ignored her.
We watched him leave, knowing how this would play,
him fetal-curled, puking, but plastic beaded.
Who can fathom what a drunk mind wants.

Still sober in Japan, I didn't know whether
to choose life or love, and so I chose both.
        I'd made an oath.
Swigging sake, I thought, *a person lives once*
and braced myself for a toilet tarantella
since nothing brings new family together
        like salmonella.
I didn't chew but swallowed the rubbery breast
and waited for the next loyalty test.

Responsory: Libera Me

from a line by Lisel Mueller

After the kill there is the feast.
After the feast there is the slumber.
Our children replace our dear deceased.
After our births we take a number.

After the toast the spirit is gone.
There's water to wine, wine into piss.
After the kiss there is the yawn
as boredom nips at the heels of bliss.

After a stumble there is flight.
After the crash there is a broom.
When we get home at the end of night,
a winter fly laps round the room.

After the glory there stirs the ash.
After the talks there is the war.
After we freeze there is the flash.
After a death, an empty drawer.

After the loss we dust the shelves.
The pictures in the box lie curled.
After we've subtracted ourselves,
no difference in the sum of the world.

After we've joined the dirt-interred,
the dusty host, the ranks of the rotten,
the nothingness we've been assured
won't come until we're long forgotten.

The Godless Month

This month the Shinto gods have left their shrines
to holiday at their annual convention,
eat rice cakes, take hot baths, and sip rice wines.
This month 8 million gods have left their shrines,
and yet our world still twirls without divines.
We wonder if they ever paid attention.
For nothing we've left sake in their shrines
while they lounge at their annual convention.

The month we held our wedding ceremony
the Shinto gods had already left the shrine.
Our priest performed the rites of matrimony
the godless month we had our ceremony—
costumes and chanting, beautiful baloney.
We're married still, but stuck in quarantine
because we held our wedding ceremony
the month the Shinto gods had left the shrine.

We offered up our prayers and chanted verses
to gods who weren't there for the ceremony.
We got the same luck, both blessings and curses,
regardless of our offerings, prayers, verses,
the mop that cleansed bad spirits—but what's worse is,
despite no gods, the priests still made their money.
We offered up the prayers and chanted verses
to family and ourselves at our ceremony.

Tanka upon Getting Married

On our wedding night,
we roll on tatami mats.
Summer rain applauds.
The whole house is our bedroom,
the whole world our home.

Small Mirror on the Kitchen Table

You left your mirror on again this morning.
The glass still held first light. Late, in a hurry,
you left behind your face, valleyed with worry
and sleeplessness. Your eyes rimmed red like warning
lights from the argument we revved last night,
yet they were still defiant, fiery.
It felt like reading someone's diary,
and I felt doubly guilty at the sight
of my own worried face floating above
your shoulder near the spice jars on the shelf—
my image scythed by your mirror's glowing scratch.
I knocked it flat, reflecting only itself.
Sipped tea. Then propped it on the sill to catch
whatever day might bring. But hoped for love.

Last Weeks in Kamino, Japan

Last week of August in Kamino,
the cedars strain to keep their green,
bell crickets and cicadas pitch
themselves against lengthening nights,
and I prepare to leave this village.
The morning after an argument,
the air inside still bruised and tender,
our pit bull, Ginger, jerks me down
the road now flanked with empty shops—
the pharmacy, bank, laundromat—
to the abandoned Shinto shrine.

Like Carmi, Illinois, the sister
town it doesn't know it has,
this town is dwindling back to nature,
slowly reclaimed by bugs and bush.
Each year the classes at the school
grow smaller, more shops shut their doors,
more empty homes gape from the hills.
The graves are overgrown because
the offspring moved to bigger towns
or no offspring remain alive.

The river here runs cold and clear
as facts—no mud, no trash, no farm sludge.
No truck exoskeletons,
no bathtubs languish on its banks.
The number that keeps washing up
is 7, the shape of its old folks,
only ones left, poking the sidewalks
with canes, always facing downward
as if searching for something lost.

In dying towns, the official color
is rust, as all equipment, pipes,
bridges, and roofs bleed back to earth
by shedding finite skins of rust.
As Carmi's empty little churches
white-dot the countryside, here
the Shinto shrines and temples are
abandoned, and this one has a sign
nailed to the wooden steps that reads
*Closed. The god has gone away
to a shrine in the next prefecture.*

Ginger and I sit on the steps.
I bend a country twelve-bar blues
that makes matchbook-sized frogs skitter
into the weeds while insects shriek
above the river's icy whisper.
Perhaps my guitar playing will call
the god back—or keep him away.
Next week my wife and I will leave
for different jobs in different towns
in Vietnam, where we'll become
one of those couples we said last year
we'd never understand. I wonder
if I'll return to Kamino,
or my old family home in Carmi,
then wonder if that's what everyone
wonders when they know they won't.

Land of the Blue Dragon

*Just outside Saigon
crowds of shoppers march through malls
where once napalm bloomed.*

Hammock Song

I've measured the world in hammocks strung
from porches, trees, and once a streetlamp
licked by high tides, where years ago
the lagoon had carried off its road.

On Wotje, an atoll where Japanese
and US forces fought by air,
land, and sea, I proposed to my wife
in Japanese for the seventh time

before she finally approved
my grammar and sincerity.
We lay together in a hammock
tied between two pandanus trees,

inches above a rising tide,
small waves unrolling like bedsheets,
a coconut toss from anti-aircraft
bunkers now reclaimed by jungle.

On the edge of a banana farm
along a bank in the Mekong Delta—
a helicopter flight from where
my father must have been stationed,

though he now has dementia, no longer
remembers me, much less the war—
we dozed on a camo-patterned hammock
as clumps of water hyacinth

floated on the river and young
snakehead fish hopped in the muck
below us, and a great blue heron
stalked mangrove shores across the river.

A drizzle pocked the henna-colored
surface with countless fist-sized Os,
figures instantly erased,
replaced, as water hyacinth

bumbled and swirled between the banks,
the same clumps drifting back and forth,
downstream at low tide, upstream at high.
We call them lucky if they get snagged

by branches, settle down, and bloom,
but like us, swinging a foot above
the current, they are rootless, wafting
free in their fixed course, yet never
emerging through the river's mouth
or returning to its muddy source.

Hanoi Tour Guide Song

In Trúc Bạch Lake, they fished out John McCain
where now young lovers smooch on paddleboat swans.
The Viet Minh shot down a fighter plane
in Trúc Bạch Lake. They fished out John McCain.
Humans, the only beings inhumane,
both torture bombers and festoon them with bronze.
In Trúc Bạch Lake, they fished out John McCain
where now young lovers smooch on paddleboat swans.

Ode to the Southeast Asian Bum Gun

Coiled like a cobra by the tank and bowl,
O bum gun, you're forever poised to strike.
Unlike Japan's Batmobile of toilets
with buttons, music, finely calibrated
water jets, warmed seats, and electric eye,
your blind, no-nonsense nozzle power-washes
butts from the cheapest bars to five-star hotels,
democratizing ass-cracks everywhere.
Hole hoser, finger fountain, keister geyser,
the first time I tried you, I gave myself
an enema. You liberate us daily
from dingleberries, save us a million rolls
of toilet paper, swaths of rainforest.

One fellow expat hated everything
in Vietnam—pollution, government,
incomprehensibly, even the food—
but he brought you back to suburban Phoenix,
his only souvenir, enthroned near his throne.
Once you clean our crack, there's no going back.

Humans evolved to walk upright yet can't
lift our noses out of each other's asses,
the deep-down reason we choose the mates we do—
we like their stink—and you make this less shameful,
your string of water massage, your anal-nozzle.
You douse our dirt-stars, polish our wrinkled pennies,
wash our winkers, scour our rusty buttons,
and when we finally rise, unburdened, we leave
with assholes dripping wet and glistening
and feeling cleaner than we could ever be.

How to Take an Afternoon Nap in Southeast Asia

If you don't have a spouse or animal in the house, borrow one.

Do not think about the plots you are plotting
or people you want to sleep with.

Your work, your troubles will still be there when you wake up.
Let them have a rest too.

If you can't find the cool spot of the pillow,
appreciate its damp warmth.

Do not let any parts of your body touch the mosquito net,
as the mosquitos will find you.

Most likely the mosquitos aren't carrying
dengue fever or malaria.

Somewhere, something in the house—the refrigerator, electric fan,
plumbing—is singing you a lullaby. Listen.

Your phone is not singing you a lullaby.
Put it in another room.

The birds, the bugs, the car horns, even the sidewalk karaoke
are all cheering you on to sleep. Let them.

Seal any anger in a glass jar and put it on a specimen shelf
with the others. You can examine it later.

Set the air conditioner or fan to make the room slightly cooler
than normal, then cover yourself with a sheet.

Do not lie in a fetal position. Casket style is better.

If a song is playing in your head (and there should always be
a song playing in your head), let it.

The car alarm drilling into your mind wants
to tunnel through your dreams. Follow it.

When trying to fall asleep, do not compose
lists or poems. If you must, wait until you wake.

At a Homestay Near Tri An Lake, I Listen to the World Breathe

From a hammock in the homestay
      someone sucks in cool night air,
           coughs, and whistles out, as if
      through ducts of sandpaper,
dark tubercular breaths.

The jungle steams in the night. Mist drifts over
      the canopy then settles into its leaves
           and fronds. Lotus flowers
      floating on the steaming black pond
exhale their powdery darkness.

Over the stone wall from the house next door,
      a transistor on the patio pulls in radio waves,
           gasps out a woman's tiny wailing song
      and then the news of riots, bombings,
war, the darkening of the world.

The world's breathing is labored. My own
      breathing is labored despite this respite
           from Hanoi smog. I used to be ambitious.
      Now, an ordinary man with a head cold,
I doze in the world's dark breaths.

From the outdoor kitchen nearby,
      coals draw oxygen from the night.
           A cauldron bubbles, exhaling stock from
      buffalo bones, onion, ginger, star anise—
sweet dark fumes lulling the world to sleep.

On a Road in Vietnam

the sun is a fist
that pounds our days
empty and flat

it grips the equator
and whips down rays
on a road that races
a canal through
a rubber tree grove

snake sunbaked
to a yellow ribbon,
frog pressed
to a bookmark, rat
flattened to a perfect
felt silhouette
of a rat—we skate

across the asphalt
from a truck's *whoosh*

we sing *we are flat!*
we are free as dead leaves
released by the banyan tree

Ode to Bui Vien, Saigon

The tourists, businessmen, backpackers, sleaze,
the middle-aged Australians, Japanese,
Americans like me, Koreans, Brits,
Chinese are siphoned through this narrow street
past bars, shops, restaurants, cafés, and clubs—
our horde squeezed through on foot and bike and bike-cart
dangling with squid and smoldering with coals,
along with pickpockets and purse snatchers,
cigarette sellers, beggars both granny and child,
and on the sidewalks stand the arm-pullers
and tummy-rubbers, sirens of massage,
the half-clad Scyllas and Charybdises
of hostess bars, smiles and ass-cheeks cloying—
slumped against the café balcony,
I watch the girls work, tireless, beautiful,
and even lovelier, the ladyboys
I'm rooting for to snare Americans
loaded with green and righteous naïvité
while dance-beats thump, battling across the street
from empty bars, lights swirling—still they come
through fish, pho, curry, barbeque, and weed,
the hungry, horny, hopeful, hopeless, drunk,
all of us lurching toward oblivion
a few paces in front of mortal fear,
till I head home, exhausted from the watching,
urine stinging already stale air,
and dawn seeps through polluted Saigon skies
like a bruise that matches ink on last drunk boys
carrying passed-out girlfriends to hotels,
last words are croaked to karaoke mics,
and last rats scuttle down foundation cracks
that smell like they lead to the end of the world,

but only till the rains wash through the street
and daylight chases out the dealers and whores
and sun sweeps out the stink then finally
sets on the hotel skyline and, once again,
on this joyless strip of bliss that's Bui Vien.

New City, Vietnam

Smoke fills the early evening.
        A field ripples with flames.
The sun sinks over the treeline
        while children shriek and play games.

Fires consume the field
        while I'm consumed with worries
for my wife and, of course,
        the beansprout that she carries.

Viets have many talents,
        but singing's not one of their gifts,
as they mutilate the tune
        yet warble heartfelt riffs

into mics and amplifiers.
        Ignoring the world's faults,
just out of fire's reach,
        an old couple dances a waltz

beneath new-planted trees
        whose leaf-tips char and singe.
This field was once a jungle
        Yanks sprayed with Agent Orange.

Now smoke from its brown grasses
        merges with Saigon smog,
the shoe factory fumes,
        grilled okra, fish, and dog.

We park our bikes in the sand,
        where the fire's less smoky and smelly.
I take my wife by the hand,
        kiss it and her pregnant belly

as we scrunch at a tiny table.
      We sip hand-pressed cane juice
poured over chunks of ice
      and watch the smoldering hues.

The western clouds are tinder
      the field and sunset ignite.
The old pair has danced and gone
      into their own good night.

Tanka Blessing for Our Baby, Not Yet Born

Do you really want
to come out into this cold,
hopeless, dying world?
If so, your mother and I
lined your bed with soft blankets.

I look in your crib,
the little white elephant
on your blue blanket.
Should you choose not to be born,
we'll keep this crib till we move.

The world's not easy.
Even some of your family
don't want to meet you.
Our home smells like fresh-baked bread
and dal. Welcome to our world.

Did you choose your name
or ask to be born? You may
not fit in this world.
But sleep. Steep. You've already
wormed your way into our hearts.

Ode to the Chom Chom

O yummy chom chom, scrumptious gremlin fruit,
in Vietnam your name means "messy hair,"
though some call you more stately rambutan.

With your green hairy spines and blood-red skin,
you're like a devil's testicles. Peel off
your leathery husk and lo! A dragon's eye—

translucent white, soft, moist, with pupil seed.
Your flesh—mild citrus, creamy-sweet, vanilla,
like your tame cousin lychee but mutated

into a tribble dreamt on psilocybin.
Carts wobble with impossible numbers of you
and navigate the narrow Viet streets

while bored street vendors croon your name to crowds
at Phú Chánh market where we bought a bag
of fifty yesterday. This afternoon

it's raining in southern Vietnam, fine rain
that streams against our windowpanes, rain pure
as a blind baby's smile, and while we sit

and watch the storm, our own newborn asleep,
we slurp and nom nom chom chom after chom chom
that spring from green water and red-orange soil

and never fill our bellies,
never let us grow tired of you who feed
our baby through his mother's milk, you who

embody Vietnam: outside that's strange,
forbidding, tender inside with a seed
hardened and primed by bitter centuries.

Milk

Back from the yellow morning fumes
of traffic, street food, and factories,
I ease open our door to find
the whole apartment smells of milk.
My wife shows me her tired smile,
while Genji nurses at her breast,
sweet milky scent mingling with warm
formula used for supplement,
the breakfast tea and coffee made
with a few dollops from mournful cows,
the homemade tofu pressed from soy milk,
coconut milk for tonight's curry.

"Daddy, what kind of milk is this?"
my daughter asked me every morning,
puzzling into her oatmeal bowl.
"Today it's crow's milk," I would say.
"I thought so! I always wondered what
crow's milk tasted like. Delicious!"
When feeding babies, there's too much time
for minds to drift into memories
or schemes like bottling Sayaka's milk
and making MILF cheese. There are enough
sad men in the US and Japan
that it could pay for Genji's college.

The neighbors down the hall are fighting
again. They need a few swigs of
unpasteurized milk of human kindness,
which has a short shelf life
and curdles with a drop of fear,
and which is why I wait until
Sayaka's finished nursing, her breasts
depleted, our baby safe asleep,

before I talk about the tests,
the enlarged prostate, possible cancer.
We don't know what to say, so I
apologize in Japanese
for being *mendokusai,* a pain.
Before we're even born, disease
and death begin suckling us,
and as adults we continue to nurse
when sleeping. Our chins tremble. Our mouths
suck nothing, lips and tongues still seeking
solace in our deepest dream-state
at dawn, that hour we fancy the world
is new and fat with innocence.

Petite chanson d'exile

I'm old enough for him to be my grandchild,
this Saigon sprout who's pulled far worlds together
though family remains unreconciled.
"I'm too old and tired to meet my grandchild,"
my mother says, each one of us exiled
across harsh seas, unlike my veteran father,
who loves but forgets the name of his grandchild,
this little one who's pulled far worlds together.

Vietnam Round

"Please wearing the mask on bus," says the sign
on the bus stop where I sit alone at 2 a.m.
Family Mart sells $2 Chilean Cabernet.
I'm dehydrated but surrounded by rain.
Frogs bark up and down the canal.
One dried, flattened frog rehydrates in the road.
My friends were already drunk when I arrived.
When friendship fails, there is wine.

My friends went home when the bar closed. No one
in our teacher group likes each other—
we just don't want to drink alone.
It's 2 a.m. and I'm drinking at the bus stop.
One of my students threw up in her mask.
I know just how she felt. Across the street,
a dog growls at the Vietcom Bank ATM.
A dried, flattened frog rehydrates in the road.

"Teacher, teacher!" she said, carrying her mask
to the bathroom like a bowl of hot soup.
When friendship fails, there's wine. When wine fails, there's song.
Frogs bark up and down the canal.
A dog whimpers at the Vietcom Bank ATM.
I know just how she felt. I'm dehydrated.
"Please wearing the mask on bus," says the sign.
Family Mart sells $2 Chilean Cabernet.

Dauber

We heard the whining through the afternoons—
the buzz and burrowing, the drone and hum.
At last I tracked down where the sound came from
and opened up the window to muddy ruins.
Mud daubers. This time last year I was stung,
their poison much more painful than paper wasps.
Along the sill, their kingdom in collapse—
mud cells chewed through by ants feasting on young.

Even at home there's no escape from war,
the horror veined through worlds hidden and small
above our son napping on the bedroom floor.
When our little god finally arose,
he squealed with laughter as Daddy sucked up all
the living and the dead through the vacuum hose.

Smiling and Waving on Lunar New Year in Quýnh Lưu, Vietnam

We hunch at a shin-high table
in child-sized plastic chairs.
The sea is black, the sky
its shroud, and waves collapse
against concrete. A group
of men and I drink beer
and many tiny cups
of rice wine—smiling, toasting
in twos, threes, the whole group—
rice wine brought in bottles
and ceramic jugs, some plain,
others infused with bananas,
snakes, bees, or monkey bones
to warm the heart and body
and increase virility.

These superstitions will outlive
the monkey, as tiger bone beliefs
have endured beyond the tiger.
Because the world cares
not if it's beautiful
or ugly, good or evil,
the superstitious scaffolding
we build to frame it, rickety
religions, will only crumble
when humans return to dust.

And my own superstitions?
If I boil the baby bottles,
array them on a clean towel
to dry in the morning sun,
will my wife be less crabby?

If I quit drinking now,
will the prostate test results
next week be negative?
Waist-deep in my fifties, I've still
not learned to stave off either
unhappiness or hope.
My life has been a string
of smiles and waves—as we age
fewer smiles, more waves—
and we are each of us
a smile and wave, ripples
on the world, and as a species,
a fading smile, a wave
collapsing back to its source.

The moon tonight has been
invisible, but we all
can feel the shift in the tide,
its tug at our blood and our bladders
as we toast one last toast
of rice wine, piss into the sea,
and wave good night, monkey bones
rattling in the bottom of the jug.

Before Leaving Vietnam

Each afternoon we nap,
listless and glistening like dumplings
in a bamboo steamer.
When the heat finally lets us up
and day says uncle to dusk,
an invisible cloud of mosquitoes
rises from the canal
to feast on ankles and foreheads,
and the breeze we've waited for
all day carries with it the tender breath
of piss and shit, sweet and sad,
a transition time, too,
for our one-year-old,
a stretch of innocence
and simplicity before the shouting
and thrown shoes, his parents
soon buffeted to separate
countries by new jobs
and COVID-19, a fractured
world that might never
drift back together again.
Come, little one. Take
your mother's hand, take mine.
Let us cross the canal
and walk in the shadows of trees
and give ourselves to dusk
and thousands of thirsty beaks.

Your Mother Still Sleeping, I Hold You Up to the Dawn

Gamecocks have barked and crowed us both awake
while sunrise throbs through clouds like a cold sore.
Mist gathers in the park where once the war
raged. No one now dares break the spell of daybreak.
Trees comb mist from the sky. From our ninth floor
apartment, I admire the foggy lake,
like green seaglass, then realize my mistake:
it's Saigon smog. Beyond the metaphor,
the view of fields and farms stretching to Saigon
is nothing if not serene this lonely hour.
Light probes the bedroom, piles of laundry, toys in
packages still. I need to shave and shower.
Instead I lift you to the blood orange dawn,
baptizing you in beauty frothed with poison.

Beachcombers

"They're never as pretty at home
as they are on the beach,"
        my wife says of the rocks
and shells as we waltz in
and out of waves, dark sands
        darkening as tide
returns. Our two-year-old
        takes all the shiny treasures
we hand him and throws
        them back to the sea without
looking at them. Perhaps
she is thinking of herself,
captured from the mountains
        and unsullied countryside
of Takachiho. Or maybe
she means us when we
        first met by our lagoon
on Majuro. No doubt
we've lost our sea-wet luster,
        worn down by a defiant toddler,
dulled by daily gratings
of each other's stubbornness.

Sayaka usually means
        more than I've considered,
but here she shows me her bounty
        in a mothered hand before
Genji tosses them back
        to tides where waves roll them,
I've counted, six waves a minute,
        3,153,600
waves a year, rolling,

rolling, rubbing, smoothing,
      wearing them smaller and smaller
to sand and then to silt,
the very sands with which
      we measure time, worn out,
dispersed as minerals
and particles back into
      the sea, particles
connecting everything
in the world, filmy solution
      giving sheen to others
before they also dissolve,
      giving sheen to us
as we step out of the sea,
our little one's small limbs
      shivering in the wind,
so we smother him with us,
the sea giving sheen to
our tired, goose-pimpled bodies,
      also dissolving and giving
momentary sheen
      to all that we hold dear.

About the Author

Richard Newman is the author of three previous books of poetry: *Borrowed Towns* (Word Press, 2005), *Domestic Fugues* (Steel Toe Books, 2011), and *All the Wasted Beauty of the World* (Able Muse Press, 2014). *Domestic Fugues* won the Steel Toe Books Formal Poetry Award. He is also the author of the novel *Graveyard of the Gods* (Blank Slate Press, 2016). His poems have appeared in *American Journal of Poetry, Best American Poetry, Boulevard, Crab Orchard Review, Literary Matters, Poetry East, Tar River Poetry,* and many other periodicals and anthologies. For over 20 years Richard served as Editor and Executive Director of *River Styx*. Currently he is Assistant Professor of Creative Writing and World Literature at Al Akhawayn University in Morocco, where he lives with his wife and son.